Dirt Simple Autoharp

by Evo Bluestein

GW00630812

Audio Contents

1 Angeline the Baker	11 St. Anne's Reel	22 Cherokee Shuffle
2 Go Tell Aunt Rhody	12 Deep Elm Blues	23 Old Molly Hare
3 My Home's Across the Blue Ridge Mountains	13 West Fork Gals	24 White House Blues
4 Old Joe Clark	14 Handsome Molly	25 Little Beggarman
5 Waterbound	15 Whiskey Before Breakfast	26 Kitchen Gal
6 Cluck Old Hen	16 Sail Away Ladies	27 Over the Waterfall
7 Soldier's Joy	17 Turkey In the Straw	28 Little Maggie
8 Susannah Gal	18 June Apple	29 Redwing
9 Bile Them Cabbage Down	19 The Girl I Left Behind Me	30 Stone's Rag
10 Policeman	20 Cripple Creek	
	21 Blackberry Blossom	

1 2

Visit us on the Web at www.melbay.com – E-mail us at email@melbay.com

Contents

Introduction

Step One – Pinch-Strum Rhythm

The songs in this book are in 4/4 or 2/4 time signature. My favorite simple strumming rhythm for this time signature is "pinch-strum, pinch-strum", or "P / P /", evenly playing each quarter note with a pinch in the lower strings (thumb and forefinger) and then a strum with the thumb moving up towards the high strings. This creates a downbeat/upbeat rhythm, where the first and third beats are always pinch and the second and fourth beats are always strum (in 4/4 time).

If you are not used to hearing or feeling four beats per measure, you will want to follow the "P / P /" line above the music notation. Of course, the notation is not always four quarter notes but rather the equivalent of four quarter notes. You will still play "P / P /", but the notation could be any combination of time values adding up to four beats per measure (half notes, eighth notes, dotted notes, etcetera).

Pinch in the bass strings on the first and third beats.

Strum with the thumb in the high strings on the second and fourth beats.

Step Two – Full Rhythm

When the "Pinch-Strum" rhythm is completely natural in your mind, you may wish to play the next variation in rhythm. Full Rhythm style is consecutive eighth notes. The "Pinch-Strum, Pinch-Strum" (P / P /) becomes "bass and strum and bass and strum and" (8 eighth notes) "b & / & b & / &". The accompanying CD features step one. For further book and video instruction, please order from evobluestein.com. Evo's Four Easy Steps MB 99187BCDEB includes the two rhythm techniques and two melody techniques

Chord Chart

For many lessons, I have included my own system for reading chord accompaniment. This is an alternative to reading the chord changes above the lyrics or in the measures of the notation. In this method, every letter name is two beats–a pinch and a strum. Thus, the first part of Soldier's Joy (8 bars) reads:

DDDD

DDA7A7

DDDD

DA7DD

How to use the Chart

If you would like to play a song in this book in G, use the I, IV, and V7 chords as designated on a song page (G, C or D7). If you would like to play the same song in the key of C (transpose), you can see in the chart that G will become C (I), C becomes F (IV), and D7 becomes G7 (V7). You can also use this chart to transpose songs from other books to keys you can play on your harp, for example, transposing from the key of E to the key of C.

Transposing Chart	Key	I	IV	V7	II7	Relative Minor
	G	G	C	D7	A7	Em
	C	C	F	G7	D7	Am
	F	F	B♭	C7	G7	Dm
	A	A	D	E7	B7	F#m
	D	D	G	A7	E7	Bm
	E	E	A	B7	F#7	C#m

Pick-up Notes

When the music has pick-up notes (incomplete measures at the beginning of some songs), you can skip playing them and begin your rhythm at the first full measure, or play a beginning full measure; but sing or count your entrance on the part of the measure where the pick-up notes begin. Listen to the CD for reference.

Transposing

When it comes to traditional fiddle dance tunes, there are keys that have been associated with certain tunes for a long time. *Soldier's Joy* is a D tune but *Old Joe Clark* is an A tune. This is more true for fiddle tunes than songs. I have placed each tune in the traditional key with which it is usually associated. The key may be changed to suit your desire, usually to accommodate your vocal range when singing is involved. Another reason might be that your autoharp doesn't have the indicated key.

Why V7?

When I teach rhythm accompaniment on other instruments I don't always use a five chord with a flatted seventh (dominant seventh). Autoharps are built with the V7 comfortably located so all the V chords in this book include a flatted seventh.

Angeline the Baker

An - ge - line the bak - er lives in our vil - lage green.—

The way I al - ways loved her beats all you've ev - er seen.———

An - ge - line the bak - er, An - ge - line the bak - er,

An - ge - line the bak - er, oh, An - ge - line the bak - er.

Angeline is handsome,
Angeline is stout.
She bakes the biscuits every morn
And pours the coffee out.

Angeline is handsome,
Angeline is tall.
She says she sprained her ankle,
Dancing at the ball.

The last time I saw her,
Was at the county fair.
Her father chased me almost home
And told me to stay there.

Angeline the baker,
Her age is twenty three.
I bought her candy by the peck
And she won't marry me.

chord chart
DDDD
DDGG
DDDD
DGDD

Go Tell Aunt Rhody

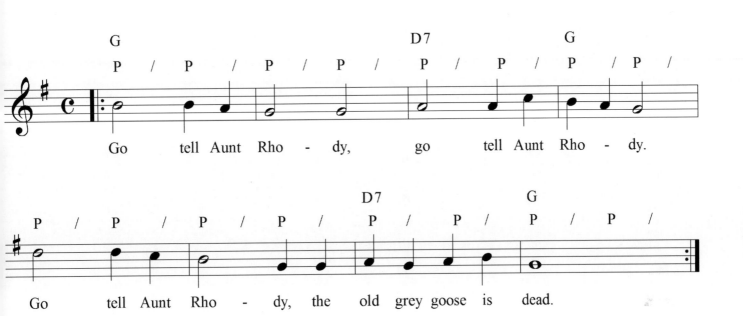

The one's she's been saving,
The one's she's been saving.
The one's she's been saving,
To make a feather bed.

She died in the millpond,
She died in the millpond.
She died in the millpond,
Standing on her head.

The goslins are weeping,
The goslins are weeping.
The goslins are weeping,
Because their mother's dead.

The old gander's mourning,
The old gander's mourning.
The old gander's mourning,
Because his wife is dead.

chord chart
GGGG
D7D7GG
GGGG
D7D7GG

7

My Home's Across the Blue Ridge Mountains

My home's a - cross the Blue Ridge Moun - tains, oh, my

home's a - cross the Blue Ridge Moun - tains. _____ My

home's a - cross the Blue Ridge Moun - tains, oh, I

nev-er ex - pect to see you an - y - more. _____

chord chart

GGGG	GGGG
GGGG	GGGG
D7D7D7D7	D7D7D7D7
GGGG	GGGG

My home's across the Blue Ridge Mountains,
My home's across the Blue Ridge Mountains.
My home's across the Blue Ridge Mountains,
Oh, I never expect to see you any more.

I'm gonna leave here Monday morning,
I'm gonna leave here Monday morning.
I'm gonna leave here Monday morning,
Oh, I never expect to see you any more.

How can I keep from crying,
How can I keep from crying.
How can I keep from crying,
Oh, I never expect to see you any more.

Rock and feed my baby candy,
Rock and feed my baby candy.
Rock and feed my baby candy,
Oh, I never expect to see you any more.

Old Joe Clark

Old Joe Clark, he had a barn, six-teen sto-ries high.

Ev-ry sto-ry in that barn was filled with chick-en pie.

Round and round— Old Joe Clark, good-bye Bet-sy Brown..

Round and round Old Joe Clark, I'm gon-na leave this town.

I went down to Old Joe's house,
Never been there before.
He slept on a feather bed
And I slept on the floor.

Sixteen horses in my team,
The leader, he is blind.
Every time the sun goes down,
There's a pretty girl on my mind.

Chorus:
Round and round Old Joe Clark,
Goodbye Betsy Brown.
Round and round Old Joe Clark,
I'm gonna leave this town.

chord chart
AAAA
AAE7E7
AAAA
AE7AA

Waterbound

Chick-ens crow-ing in the old pine tree, chick-ens crow-ing in the old pine tree. Chick-ens crow-ing in the old pine tree, way down in North Car-o-lin - a.

Get up Charlie, let's go home,
Get up Charlie, let's go home
Get up Charlie, let's go home,
Before the water rises.

Waterbound and I can't get home,
Waterbound and I can't get home.
Waterbound and I can't get home,
Way down in North Carolina.

Stay all night and don't go home,
Stay all night and don't go home.
Stay all night and don't go home,
Stay with me till morning.

10

Cluck Old Hen

Track 6

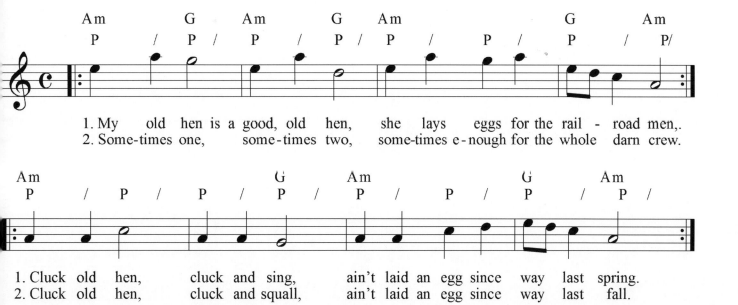

1. My old hen is a good, old hen, she lays eggs for the rail - road men,.
2. Some-times one, some-times two, some-times e-nough for the whole darn crew.

1. Cluck old hen, cluck and sing, ain't laid an egg since way last spring.
2. Cluck old hen, cluck and squall, ain't laid an egg since way last fall.

My old hen's a good old hen,
She lays eggs for the railroad men.
Sometimes one, sometimes two,
Sometimes enough for the whole darn crew.

Chorus:
Cluck old hen, cluck and sing,
Ain't laid an egg since way last spring.
Cluck old hen, cluck and squall,
Ain't laid an egg since way last fall.

My old hen's a good old hen,
She lays eggs for the railroad men.
Sometimes eight, sometimes ten,
That's enough for the railroad men.

The first time she cackled, she cackled in the lot,
The next time she cackled, she cackled in the pot.
The first time she cackled, she cackled in the stable,
The next time she cackled, she cackled on the table.

Had a little hen, she had a wooden leg,
Best old hen that ever laid an egg.
She laid more eggs than any hen around the barn,
Another drink of cider wouldn't do us any harm.

chord chart

AmGAmG	AmAmAmG
AmAmGAm	AmAmGAm
repeat	*repeat*

Soldier's Joy

I love somebody, yes, I do,
I love somebody, yes, I do.
I love somebody, yes, I do,
Betcha five dollars that you can't guess who.

Dance all night and fiddle all day,
Dance all night and fiddle all day.
Dance all night and fiddle all day,
That's the soldier's joy they say.

chord chart
DDDD   DDGG
DDA7A7   DDA7A7
DDDD   DDGG
DA7DD   DA7DD
repeat   *repeat*

Susannah Gal

Fly a-round my— pret-ty, lit-tle miss,— fly a-round my dais-y.

Fly a-round my— pret-ty, lit-tle miss, you— al-most drive me craz-y.

Fly around my pretty, little miss, fly around my daisy,
Fly around my pretty, little miss, you almost drive me crazy.

You can't stay here if you can't shuck corn, Susanannah,
You can't stay here if you can't shuck corn, Susanannah Gal.

Rock into my notion, now, Susanannah,
Rock into my notion, now, Susanannah Gal.

chord chart

DDDD	DDGD
A7A7DD	DDA7A7
DDDD	DDGD
A7A7DD	DA7DD
repeat	*repeat*

Bile Them Cabbage Down

I wish I had a nick - el, I wish I had a dime.

I wish I had a pret-ty lit-tle girl to kiss and call her mine.

Bile them cab - bage down boys, bake them hoe-cakes round. The

on - ly song that I could sing was bile them cab - bage down.

	Chorus:	chord chart
Possum up a 'simmon tree,	Bile them cabbage down boys,	AADD
Raccoon on the ground.	Bake them hoecakes round.	AAE7E7
Raccoon told the possum,	The only song that I could sing was	AADD
Shake them 'simmons down.	Bile them cabbage down.	AE7AA

If I had a needle and thread,   I went across the mountains,
Fine as I could sew.   I crossed them in the spring.
I'd sew my gal to my coat tail,   I got on the other side,
And down the road I'd go.   You could hear my banjo ring.

Policeman

Shoot your dice and have your fun this morn-ing.

Shoot your dice and have your fun this morn-ing. Shoot your dice and

have your fun, run like the de-vil when the po-lice come this morn-ing.

Shoot your dice and have your fun this morning,
Shoot your dice and have your fun this morning.
Shoot your dice and have your fun,
Run like the devil when the police come this morning.

Two little children lying in the bed this morning,
Two little children lying in the bed this morning.
Two little children lying in the bed,
One rolled over to the other and said, "Good morning."

Bullfrog jumped from bank to bank this morning,
Bullfrog jumped from bank to bank this morning.
Bullfrog jumped from bank to bank,
Skinned his ol' back from shank to shank this morning.

I know something I ain't gonna tell this morning,
I know something I ain't gonna tell this morning.
I know something I ain't gonna tell,
I want to go to heaven in a coconut shell this morning.

chord chart
AAAA
AAAA
DDDD
AAAA
DDDD
AAAA
AAAA

St. Anne's Reel

Deep Elm Blues

If you go down to Deep Elum,
Keep your money in your shoes.
The women in Deep Elum,
Got those Deep Elum Blues.

If you go down to Deep Elum,
Take your money in your pants.
The women in Deep Elum,
Won't give the men a chance.

Now once I knew a preacher,
Preached the Bible through and through.
He went down into Deep Elum,
Now his preaching days are through.

chord chart
DDDD
DDDD
DDDD
DDD7D7

GGGG
GGGG
DDDD
A7A7A7A7
A7A7A7A7
DDDD

17

West Fork Gals

Track 13

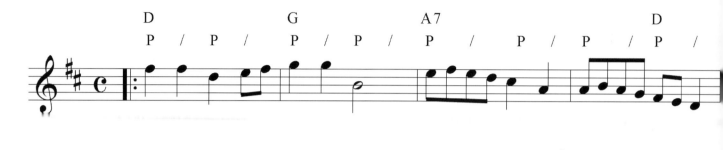

chord chart

DDGG	DDDD
A7A7A7D	A7A7A7A7
DDGG	A7A7DD
A7A7A7D	DA7DD
repeat	*repeat*

Handsome Molly

I wish I was in London,
Or some other seaport town.
I'd set my foot in a steamboat
And sail the ocean round.

While sailing o'er the ocean,
While sailing o'er the sea.
I'd think of Handsome Molly,
Wherever she may be.

She rode to church on Sunday,
She passed me on by.
I saw her mind was changing,
By the rovin' of her eye.

Don't you remember Molly,
When you give me your right hand.
You said if you'd ever marry,
That I would be the man.

Now you broke your promise,
Go home with who you please.
While my poor heart is aching,
You're lying at your ease.

Her hair was black as a raven,
Her eyes were black as coal.
Her cheeks were like lilies,
Out in the morning grown.

chord chart
GGGG
GGD7D7
D7D7GG
CCGG

19

Whiskey Before Breakfast

chord chart

DDDD	DDDD
GDA7A7	A7A7A7A7
DDDD	DA7GD
GDA7D	GDA7D
repeat	*repeat*

Sail Away Ladies

Ev-er I get my new house done, sail a-way lad-ies, sail a-way.

Give my old one to my son, sail a-way lad-ies, sail a-way.

Don't she rock 'em, di-de-o, don't she rock 'em di-de-o.

Don't she rock 'em, di-de-o, don't she rock 'em, di-de-o.

Come along boys and go with me,
Sail away ladies, sail away.
We'll go back to Tennessee,
Sail away, ladies, sail away.

I got a letter from Shilo town,
Sail away ladies, sail away.
Big St. Louis's burning down,
Sail away ladies, sail away.

Come along children, don't you cry,
Sail away ladies, sail away.
You'll be angels by and by,
Sail away ladies, sail away.

Chorus:
Don't she rock 'em, di-de-o,
Don't she rock 'em, di-de-o.
Don't she rock 'em, di-de-o,
Don't she rock 'em, di-de-o.

chord chart
AAE7A
AAAA
repeat

AADD
DDAA
AAE7E7
E7E7AA
repeat

21

Turkey In the Straw

Well, I went to the riv-er but I could-n't get a-cross so I jumped on the back of an old blind horse.— He would-n't go for-ward and he would-n't stand still,— he went up and down like an old saw mill.— Tur-key in the straw, tur-key in the straw. Tur-key in the hay,— tur-key in the hay. Well, the old folks danced with their moth-er-in-law,— sing a lit-tle song called tur-key in the straw.—

Did you ever go fishing on a bright sunny day
And you're standing on a log and the log rolls away.
With your hands in your pockets and your pockets in your pants,
You watch the little fishies do the hoochie-koochie dance.

I went to Cincinnati and I walked around the block
And I walked right into a doughnut shop.
I handed the lady a five-cent piece
And I pulled two doughnuts right out of the grease.

She looked at the nickel and she looked at me,
She said this nickel's no good to me.
There's a hole in the middle and it's all the way through,
Says I there's a hole in the doughnut too.

chord chart

GGGG	GGGG
GGD7D7	CCCC
GGGG	GGGD7
GGD7G	GGD7G
repeat	*repeat*

June Apple

I— wish I was a June— ap - ple,—

hang-in'— on a— tree.————— Ev-'ry— time my true love passed she'd

take a lit - tle bite of me.

I wish I was a June apple,
Hangin' on a tree.
Every time my true love passed,
She'd take a little bite of me.

Peaches in the summertime,
Apples in the fall.
If I don't get that pretty little girl,
I don't want none at all.

chord chart

AAAA	AAAA
GGAA	GGDD
AAAA	AAAA
AGAA	GGAA
repeat	*repeat*

The Girl I Left Behind Me

chord chart

GGCC   GGGG
GGD7D7   GGD7D7
GGCC   GGCC
D7D7GG   D7D7GG
repeat   *repeat*

Cripple Creek

chord chart

AADA	AAAE7
AAE7A	AAE7A
AADA	*repeat*
AAE7A	
repeat	

Blackberry Blossom

chord chart

GD7CG	EmEmEmD7
CGGD7	EmEmGD7
GD7CG	EmEmEmD7
CGD7G	CGD7G
repeat	*repeat*

Cherokee Shuffle

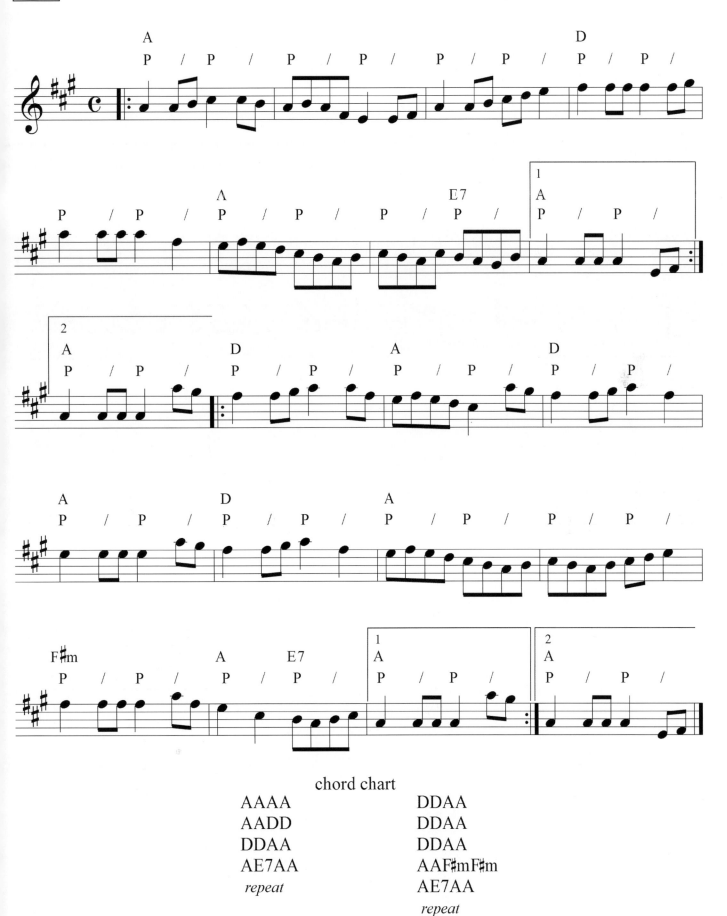

chord chart

AAAA	DDAA
AADD	DDAA
DDAA	DDAA
AE7AA	AAF#mF#m
repeat	AE7AA
	repeat

Old Molly Hare

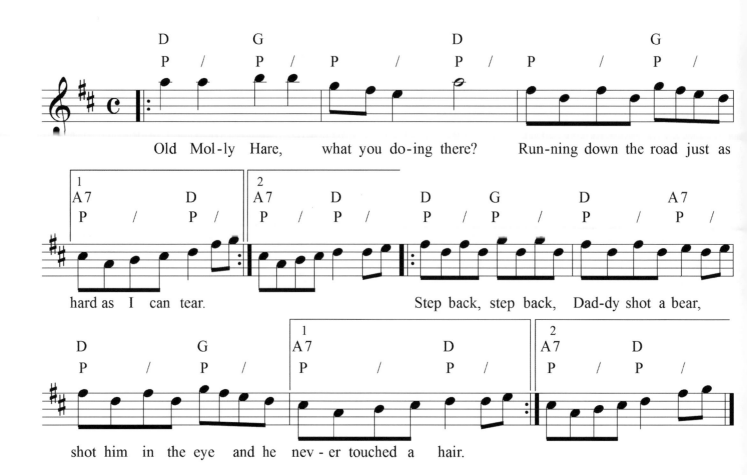

Old Mol-ly Hare, what you do-ing there? Run-ning down the road just as hard as I can tear. Step back, step back, Dad-dy shot a bear, shot him in the eye and he nev-er touched a hair.

Old Molly Hare what you doing there?
Running down the road just as hard as I can tear.
Run down one, run down two,
Run down one and I give it to you.

Step back, step back, Daddy shot a bear,
Shot him in the eye and he never touched a hair.
Old Molly Hare what are you doing there?
Sitting by the roadside chewing on a bear.

chord chart
DGGD
DGA7D
repeat

DGDA7
DGA7D
repeat

White House Blues

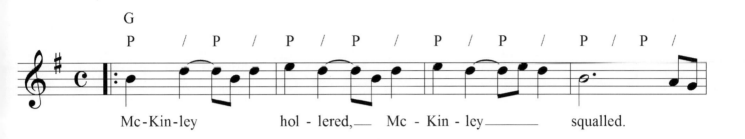

McKinley hollered, McKinley squalled.

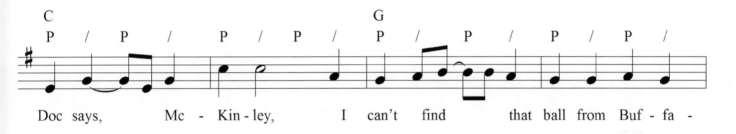

Doc says, McKinley, I can't find that ball from Buffalo

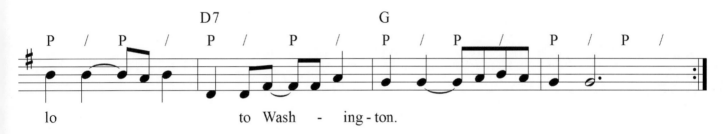

lo to Washington.

McKinley hollered, McKinley squalled.
Doc says, McKinley, I can't find that ball
From Buffalo to Washington.

Roosevelt in the White House, he's doing his best,
McKinley in the graveyard, he's taking his rest.
He is gone a long, long time.

Hush up little children, now don't you fret,
You'll draw a pension at your papa's death.
From Buffalo to Washington.

Roosevelt in the White House, drinking out of a silver cup,
McKinley in the graveyard, he'll never wake up.
He is gone a long, long time.

Ain't but one thing that grieves my mind,
That is to die and leave my poor wife behind.
I'm gone a long, long time.

Look here you little children, rest your breath,
You'll draw a pension at your papa's death.
From Buffalo to Washington.

Standing at the station, just looking at the time,
See if I could run it by half past nine.
From Buffalo to Washington.

Train, that train, she's just on time,
She'll run a thousand miles from eight o'clock to nine.
From Buffalo to Washington.

Yonder comes the train, she's coming down the line,
Blowing every station, Mr. McKinley's a dying.
It's hard times, it's hard times.

Look here, you rascal, you see what you've done,
You shot my husband with that Iver Johnson gun.
Get back to Washington.

Doctor on the horse, he tore down his mane,
Said to that horse, you got to outrun that train.
From Buffalo to Washington.

Doctor a running, took off his specs,
Said Mr. McKinley, you better pass in your checks.
You're bound to die, you're bound to die.

Little Beggarman

chord chart

AAAD AAAD   GGGD AAAD
AAGG AE7AA   AAGG AE7AA
repeat   *repeat*

Kitchen Gal

chord chart

AGAA	AmGAmAm
AGE7E7	AmAmAmAm
AGAA	AmGAmAm
GE7AA	AmGAmAm
repeat	*repeat*

Over the Waterfall

chord chart

DA7DD   DGDD
DA7DD   DA7DD
DA7DD   DGDD
CCGG   DA7DD
repeat   *repeat*

Little Maggie

chord chart

Oh, yonder stands Little Maggie,
With a dram glass in her hand.
She's passing by her troubles
And a-courtin' another man.

How can I ever stand it,
For to see those two blue eyes,
A-shining like a diamond,
Like a diamond in the skies?

Now it's march me down to the station,
With my suitcase in my hand.
I'm going away to leave you,
I'm going to some far distant land.

GGGG
FFD7D7
GGD7D7
GGGG

I would rather be in some lonesome holler,
Where the sun could never shine.
Then to know you're another man's darling
And no longer a darling of mine.

Sometimes I have one nickel,
Sometimes I have one dime.
Sometimes I have ten dollars
Just to pay Little Maggie's fine.

Pretty flowers was made for blooming,
Pretty stars was made to shine.
Pretty girls was made for a boy's love,
Surely Maggie was made for mine.

33

Redwing

Stone's Rag

About the Author

photo: Michael Melnyk

Evo Bluestein is known for his music on many instruments but he has a special connection to the autoharp. Perhaps the highest recognition of this is his 2009 induction into the Autoharp Hall of Fame.

His style of playing is greatly influenced by the late autoharp master Kilby Snow and Evo is known as the foremost player of this old-time style. Evo's book and DVD, "Autoharp in Four Easy Steps", are among the most popular instruction methods available today. Evo has also developed two successful and popular brands of autoharp, the "Evoharp®" and the ¾ sized "Sparrowharp®".

In addition to helping many adults learn music on the autoharp for over thirty years, children in numerous schools have learned to play and sing using the autoharp in programs that Evo has implemented. In response to the terrific reviews of his rendition of "Troubles" on the Autoharp Legacy CD, Evo completed an album of songs and tunes, titled "Off the Top". He is also an accomplished dance caller, teaching folk dance as an independent contractor throughout California schools. Evo is co-founder of the California Autoharp Gathering.

Ordering Information

The Evoharp custom autoharp

The Sparrowharp 3/4 sized harp

For more information about products and Evo's performance and workshop schedules, visit www.evobluestein.com.